ADJY

ADJY

by
Michael J. Stuckey Jr.

"Stuckey Publishing"

Short Note

Titled: Adjy, consist of 145 poems of Treacherous, Deceptive, & significant Poetry. The Impression Is not just of the Righting Style. From the beginning through to the end, understanding you will have. While reading or when finished reading this book of poetry: Adjy.

ABOUT THE AUTHOR

Born in the summer of 1977, Michael began writing emotionally torturous writing's & poetry as a child. He spent 19 long yrs in Tile & Stone industry becoming a master stonesman and installer, then forced to retire from the exceptional career he had built in 2008. Since that time, Michael became a Published Author / Writer of several Poetry books, recipe books, and realistic fiction novels.

Main Website: Author-MStuckey.com

Poetry Index

CONTENTS

Acknowledgment

The poem "Navy Cheer" is dedicated to the memory of John J. Cuff Sr. a Father and a Friend.

General

Blessed

People praise or slander,
Quickly we become.
Envied we are by the Gods,
Though we fall far and hard.
Privileged are we,
For we're not cursed with eternity.

Evolution

Once to have risen by rite of blood,
As are the Gods of the Old Religion,
Counts, Earls, Dons, Noblemen and Kings,
Quickly come to rise,
Yet no differently forgotten.

Of Champions

Activist do what's right,
Thugs live by Honor, Pride and Respect,
Revolutionaries take care of their own,
Freedom Fighters peruse justice by any means,
Minding their place and
Never stick our nose in other people's business,
Lands of Political Governing
Call us Terrorist.

Soldier's Medals

Weigh-in heavy on their backs,
Once Proudly worn on their chest.
Shamed on by the People,
Locked drawer and dust covered,
Their Gleam and Sparkle
No longer to be seen.

Truth of Freedom

Our thoughts of it vanished,
Writings of it only in ancient scrolls,
Site of it, only left in our dreams,
Spoken words of it Role off our tongues, no
more,
Shown only by actions,
Now called treason,
Against a country of States United.

Request:

Morbid inhibitions,
Discreet insurrection.
White rose petal bath,
Classic jazz by candle light.
Fire in her eyes of notions abiding,
Goddess Ti's I, who called you down.

Between Couples

While lying aching & annoyed,
Their painful pleasures a void,
Suspenseful twisted life,
Of eyes from romance,
A couples words,
Written in the Book of Torment,
They awake to find the sun is shining.

Prized ornament:

Still waters of a heart once broken,
Chains of emotion entangle,
Temptation of soigne,
Your Love is baneful,
Prisoner now graven,
Will you keep me?

Lying on

Delicate touch of rose petals,
Gentle persuasion grazing inner thigh,
Perfume in a sultry night,
Sinful chattels,
Of a significant requite.

Even in dreams

Your essence burns bright,
Perception of depths in your writings,
Being seduced by an endless look,
In awkward possibility.

Apposing Romance

Epiphyllous Orchid opening,
Thriving 'n' showing its beauty.
Striving to kiss the moon's glow,
Filled with passion 'n' love,
In-captivating.

Set aside your doubts, your fears,
Your contradicting mind,
Ti's a Muse I found in Thea,
Curiously intrigued yet speechless,
As my breath escapes me.

Not Right

Your convictions of Lies,
Spilled over tea & coffee,
Truth of you,
Aired over the internet,
Convinced in denial,
Optimistic,
For what you want.
Relishing,
For what you have,
For what you've done....

Rocked

Depths
Of Intrinsic beauty.
Supported, rocked mortality.
Transitions of hell.
Defecation of one.
Misspoken ritual.

Equivalent

Enticed & accomplished,
An Acknowledged Person of Note,
Unacquainted bounds,
Misery continued,
Of happiness stain,
Yet remain an Erotic Clout.

Returned

Through the gates,
Rode the serpent,
Marvelous wonders,
Eyes gouged out,
By wet kiss sent back,
Excuses no more,
A reasonable Alibi,
Yet known to me.

Cause

Lingering Souls
Venues of life
Clouded perceptions
Socially innate
Privately versatile
Reason of none
The vindication of one....

Unknowing

Trying morally proper.
Insignificant to others,
Thus endeavors.
Ti's will as you implore,
Is I that invoke,
Of thy bidding you have done....

Answer

Got bills paid,
Good times to have,
Every one in my life hates me,
Yet everyone feels safe with me.
You're all welcome.
I have what I want, when I want It,
Only the wicked just don't care.

Numb

Anything good enough for tonight,
Acting like a stumbling ass,
Any reason to fight,
Forgot how to go home,
Taxi ride, Can't think.

Finally don't feel,
Numb 'n' Drunk again.

Effective

Trickling streams,
Sparkles of crystal,
Scriptures imposed,
Heavy lays the heart.
Treatment replenishing,
Personal conversing,
Effective meads,
As to a beaver dam.

Clergy

15 minutes,
Virtues exposed,
39. Notes,
No strings attached,
Obligations confined,
Certificate of Religious Anarchy,
As a Clergy,
Licensed to Wed.

Cardinal

Piece of grass,
Blade of straw,
Leafs knitted together,
Beautifully colored,
Almost graceful,
Fluttering wings weave,
Their Basket.
With eggs to come,
Fall is no more,
Spring's finally come.

Cat's Gift

Experience to share,
Black of a mortals being.
Lessons to teach,
On the backs of long winged thing.
Entranced placed,
Inevitable grief.
Taught in expression,
One's aspirations.

Washed Away

Houses damaged,
Some completely gone.
Laugh as they Pray,
Destruction by mayhem.
Diseased replaced belongings,
Mold unstoppably growing.
Keepsakes & momentos,
Now a memory.
Tens of hundreds of
People's lives washed away,
Thanks Absentee Higher Being.

Arranged

Pleasures of quaint
Gleaming night stars,
Withering in flight,
Cordial invite,
Married at first sight,
Locked by vows,
In a lost Night.

Infinity

Rotting Corpses come to pass,
Before time 'n' during life,
Evolution in space,
As worlds revolve,
Our Souls,
Belong to Each Other.

Photograph

Perfect replica capturing moments,
Of sorrow & happiness.
From shades of black & white,
Now brilliant colors,
Depicting day or night,
Essence of Exquisite Moments.

Referred

Company by the order,
To leave not to stay.
Services rendered,
Couldn't feel better,
Found in pleasure,
Satisfaction,
As the Door Closes.

Drought

Brown & gray,
Withered away,
Wilted everything,
Cold Winter's Morning,
Dying gloomy drought.

Let Go

Fixation of Infatuation,
Life never knew.
Fear of chance lost,
Latched on with might,
Scarred from site.
No matter what say?
What duo or how try,
Already lost,
This Invisible Fight.

Season's Love

As Spring we meet,
Summer coming find wear falling,
August of love.
Time away to our selves,
Not even a thought.

Annoyed & overwhelmed,
Brings fall's arguments.
With resentment comes winter.

Hatred sets in,
Desolate cold of February,
Breakups begin.

April warms the heart,
Feel of changing,
To Get Back Together Again.

Torn Tree

Torn dead branch,
Ties of heartache,
Who I used to be.
Lightning split Walnut Tree,
Ability diminished,
Alive & thriving branch,
Of who you
Believed I Could Be.

Quiet Surface

Cold & clear
Quick current
Iron feet
Wildly seductive
Intelligent receptive,
Violent yet delicate
Last night's red head
River deep

Heaven

They say the stairway to heaven
Lies within a woman's eyes
That's nothing but a lie
It lies between her thighs.

They say these lies
To keep us from the prize
To get things done
Out of despise.
For we came from it
We're dying to get back in it.

So we tell them
We see the stairway in their eyes.

While

Looking for Ease of mind Calmed.
Looking for What have known Never?
Looking for Return of what never Felt.
Looking for Tormented day Without.
Looking for Taste of blissful Liven.
Looking for A wealthy Life.

Empathy

In the mirror void of pain
Non empathetic for the
Need of You to need of Me,
Keeping me sane.

Fade away in brake waters,
On shore's edge.
Sigh over You,
Just as well aware,
A stranger looks back at me
Nothing is Fine.

Smokes

Craving compels you,
Stress engages.
Desire captivates you,
Endorphins Compensate.

Thoughts trap you,
Temper rages.
The addiction consumes you,
Violent outburst may become you.
Subconsciously never leaves you.

Quitting Cigarettes,
What a Miserable, Loyal Bitch.

Significant

Inside

The end of love,
Only true disease of one's soul.
Though we push forward,
We are eternally scared.
No different than a quivering child.
Crying on the inside,
a last resort,
Protecting One's Self.

Affable

Poverty & sickness,
Misery & worthlessness,
If you're ruled by regret,
Despair you shall.
You'll die as you lived.
No acknowledgment.

A Peasant Slave in life, as in Death,
Never to have been, Never to be.

What It Takes

Determination, confidence,
Lust & desire,
Surely you'll be caught,
A clumsy homicide it will be.

Street smarts,
Adversity, intelligences,
Patience, conviction,
Control, restraint,
Adapt & learn your commonsense.
No evidence, no witness.
The skill to get away with it,
A carrier you've now made.

Lost Path

Eats as a slob sending his army to war,
With his entitlement, Gluttony
He can afford no Couth.
Honor pushes the men charging in,
As wine & juices of fat run down his chin.
The soldiers sent to be massacred,
Allowing them only the righteousness of
intent,
Deprived from the glory of an honorable
death,
All for Corrupt kings & or Presidents.

Navy Cheer

Rat Shit, Cat Shit,
Dirty old Twat,
69 Douche bags Tied in a Knot,
Mother Fucker, Cock Sucker,
Gobble Gobble Chew,
I'm an A. B. ,
What the Fuck Are You?

In The Cards

Deprived of retribution,
Of past ambition,
Was told let alone,
Police & government will handle it.
I let it be, but not forgotten.

For them a Political Year,
Cruciate as can be,
Police tried to frame Thee.
Inadequate at their bluff,
Dragging their feet,
With Indictments pending,
Prosecutors hands tied.

Tis I, Forced to Do Nothing.
Associates & Affiliates Looking Down upon
Thee,
Worried where I stand.
No longer a Reckoned Individual.
Balance of Thy life,
Being played with a shitty
Politician's Poker Hand.

Insanity

Get up at 3 Am,
Work 16 hours a day,
For minimum wage,
Only to come home to:
The same slop I had the night before,
To listen to Her mouth over bull shit,
Then to clean the house.... cause she's tired,
To take a cold shower,
Every day, for 50 years.

Finally to Retire:
A life you've worked your whole Life for,
To have any kind of Life.
That which you broke your ass for,
Only to be.
Too Old, Decrepit & Sick,
With a little savings to enjoy it.
Praying & Begging,
You Will Die With Some Dignity.

Controversy

One can not say,
To be defined.
How it is their protection,
Of self defense.

Their negligence.
According to their Law,
With Contradictions & Penal Code.

It's our right To Bear Arms.

Carnage

Done in past lives
Pay for in events leading to death.
Reborn we remember
Shaping our current life.
What we choose life after life
Only to suffer at the end of each cycle
Repeating till we perfect.

Called

Hypocrites preaching to cover up,
Government corruption to hide Their greed,
Sticking their nose where it doesn't belong,
To hide war with every one,
Conclusive of conflict,
Politics Known as,
Nations United.

Altar Boy

As the Priest Blessed the Child,
Gleamed with a smile.
Gazing down upon baby Boy,
Anticipation in angst.
For when He becomes an Altar Boy.

Priest says,
"I Now Bless You My Child"

Years gone by,
Tears we've all cried.
Now Lead Altar boy.

Once again the Priest
Looks upon Him at waist height,
While parting His hair,

the Priest States,
"Allow Me to Bless You My Son.
With the Juices of Life,
When I'm finished I'll get you a Towel."

"You are now twice blessed,
Pennants are next."

Religion

Outed & caught. the Priest cries
With bloody whipped eye's,
Pope & Archbishop,
Keeping funds abounding.
Relocation a must,
Pendants of prayer,
Punishment only in trust.

Moved to Child's, Ohio.
New identity increasing profits.
To fund & support
The next Child Molester,
From Bridge Port.

Entanglement of positions,
In public or behind closed doors,
Different names, different ladies,
Some have cute designer trim,
Some smooth as silk,
Each time an exhibition.
Some sensual,
Some a taste for BDSM,
Others simply erotic.

When she is satisfied,
I'm done,
If not satisfied,
Mix Techniques & Continue.

Tiers

Wondered by one, noticed by all.
Curious why I fall,
Brilliant design,
Stature crumbles,
Segregation,
Not by Color, Not by Clout,
Financial discrimination,
Tier of society all too soon fall.

Erased

Withered & frail looking back,
Each ring a twist of years pass.

Happiness,
As breakaway moments,
Sorrow times cling to bark.
Darker peaces telling age,

Wilted life's vine.
Striped in to string,
Used for many of things,
History of One's Past.

Nobility

Once infatuated, learned emotions.
Once fell in love, lost my self.
Now; have known regret.
As the Author of Poetry books
Partly handicap.
A House I can't stand.

Soon to come
An Apartment Building,
A Laundromat,
Car Wash.

Bread for business,
Not for subtleties of Family.
Loveless & wealthy
Papers of Entitlement
Once a Lord, Now a Nobleman,
Craving the life of a family man,

A wish to have what I've never known.

Retired

Delinquently Quaint of Love's Hate,
Drifting on Rivers of Nights Pass.
Inartistic Beauty,
Break of Day on Shore's Edge.
Gentile rip currents behind,
Blanketed Stars cover Me,
Wrapped in a Cloudy Mist,
Ineffectual & Intellectual rapids ahead.
Will know of no Bliss.

Analogy

To right one's Past,
Tis to suffer in Torment.
Feelings of past come To Light,
Thoughts now hinder everything In Sight.
Notion of what was to what Is,
Now clawing at You,
Tearing Pieces away Each Time,
Till nothing but What,
Been Written Remains.

Reflections

While opening doors
In a hall full of doors
To find my self
To find the way
Entering each entrance
Forced to view
Moments of the past.

Not just of thy latest life ended
Rather; of all past lives
To remember steps taken
To see your mistakes
To find the way to your next life
Along the way, to understand.

Vague Memory

Flared Cuffs,
Over Coat Vest,
Panache Taste,
Proper Etiquette,
Stone & Bolder Houses,
Cottages for Servants,
Peasants for Amusement,
1861; an Aristocrat's Life.

Patient's Appreciation

Hear at Progressions,
Delicate Hands forcing to bend.
Poked, Prodded, Twisted & even Pressed.
Seemingly amused they are,

With Dictated Positions,
This is no place for Shy Inhibitions.
With Painful Acts not of Pleasure.
Applied movements,
Leading Us from Stiff Painful Ache,
To Flexibly at Ease.
Now we can move,
Even if only For a Little While.

For Reducing the Stiff,
Aching Annoyance of Our Day,
Your Unwavering Persistence.
We Thank You,
For Giving us back, Our Dignity.

White Lies

We do it to protect one's feelings,
We do it to protect someone,
We do it to protect our selves,
Sometimes to avoid exposure,
We do it to get what we want,
We do it to get out of trouble,
We do it when it's convenient
Or suits our needs,
Sometimes with good intentions,
Sometimes for the wrong reasons,
Sometimes it is a reaction,
Not always meant to hinder,
Little White Lies,
Cast a web of deceit.

Sitting Stone

Like a Mile Stone,
Trucking State to State,
Trying to get Home,
Applause One's Character Flaws,
70 & Cruising.
State Line Lost from my Sight,
Driving all Night,
Passing Cars like Sitting,
Pond Stones,
Mile after Ripple,
Hand on the Wheel,
Till I get Home.

Glass Stones

Mistaken Foresight,
Inevitable view,
Shattered Emotions,
Of a Cast Stone.
Seen through Pane Glass Doors,
Momentary lapses in Self Confidence,
Doors of Future Options,
Cast Stones,
Eliminating Doors,
Shattering like life's past.

Desire

Only when Single, Is to be Empty.
Only when In Love, Is to come Alive.
Only to See, When Looking.
Only to Feel, When Touched.
Only to Hate, When Inflicted Upon.
Only to have Emotions, When Finally
Complete.
If Only To Bleed, When Cut.

A Soldier

I hear them at Night,
I see them in the Light,
Difference as they Move away,
Clearer as they come closer,
I can tell their Country, Clan,
Or If, With what Gang,
Even the ones well paid.
Some by their Eyes,
Or by their Stature.
Some by their Accents,
Or by their Colors,
If they're coming for Me,
Or just passing by.

No Matter from which we came,
Nor for what We Fight for,
Justified or Not.
What is Our Payment?
Whether it be Honor, Respect,
Family, Land, Country or Money.
We all have 4 things in common,
No longer who we were.
Don't know what we've become.
We all are Soldiers,
& We All Want to Come Home.

Uncle

They turn to you when in Doubt,
In Trouble & even when they sneak out.
They confide in you, Look up to you,
They come to you instead of their Parents,
Trust & Rely on you....

You get to help them, teach them,
Protect them & yes you get to spoil them,
Get them wound up & on a sugar high,
Then send them home.
How great it is Being an Uncle.

Bound To Be

Declaration of independence
Gives us the right to be who we are.
Constitution allows us to
Live by: honor, pride 'n' dignity.
What's right, now lost to the people.

Man's laws revoke your rights of freedom
Populous governed by politics & greed.
Economy collapsing,
Our constitution rescinded.
Communist country we're becoming.

Audacity

We fight for what's right,
Different it may be to each one of us.
We fight to prosper & obtain,
Achieve what others before us could not.
We fight for our honor 'n' our pride,
For our very existence.
We fight for politicians,
Who start wars over greed 'n' oil.
We fight claiming freedom,
In protection of the people back home.
While forcing our ways on them.
Society shrugs their shoulders, rolls their eyes
Informing us of their disapproval.
Still we fight for all of these and so much more.

Continued Deception

Sluggish

Slow forgiveness.
Orchid of Orange, bold Yellow Stripe.
Amazing Structure.
Move Sluggish not to Avoid.
Inviting Eyes, Moments lost.
Breathless of Elegant way.
Optional,
Will it be Maybe ?

Kind Eyes

Wrong Places Looked for Love.
In Your Eyes Something
I've Never seen.
In your Eyes Like,
A Dream.
Your Touch,
Delicate as an Orchid Petal,
Sensual way of a Rose.
Devastating,
To find what it is You Want.

UN-Replied

Gazing into each others Eyes,
Words of Ernest Spoken,
Want Your Mind,
Want Your Heart,
Want Your Soul,

Replying,
Falling In love with You,
Want All of You,
Want Everything with You,

While an Empty Look,
Lies on My Face & No Words Spoken.
Turned Down & Looked Away,
In Awkward Confusion.

We May

Hand in Mine,
Walking through the Night.
Gentle Persuasion,
Fingers Grazing Inner Thigh.

True to Thy Self,
Led by Romance,
Love Prevails,
Can not be bound.

Us is a Sin,
I'd Have no other way.
With Promises of nothing,
Fruitful Outlook.

Bright Essence

By Reality,
Perceptions Distorted,
Of Individual Depths,
Enlightenment of Past,
Your Essence Burns Bright,
Seduced,
The Moment is Now,
Possibility is Endless.

As You

Only one to believe in me,
Tried to be what You wanted.
When finally trusted by You,
Shortcomings & failures
All you received.
There's Nothing I wouldn't do,
Kill, Maim, Massacre,
Even Be Measurable Barely holding on.
As You ,
I wish I could believe
For You,
I will Live.

You're Still

Your Image,
Words you've Spoken to me.
Moments You fled scared,
Hid from Your.

To come back for Happiness,
To show me You believe,
To feel like a Woman,
To show me You want, With Me.
To be wanted & Known,
Only to pull away,
Playing childish games.

Ended & Lost
Of your Memory,
You're Still Haunting me.

After All

You were the One,
What of all,
You've put me through.
Forgiveness,
I hold for You.
Still after all,
Fear you're the One
I would wait a life time for.

Bait

Showed me a life,
Life I never knew.
Introduced me to hope,
Compassion,
something more than Just.

Like Bait on a Fish Hook,
Dangled Possibility.
No Matter how hard,
Sink my teeth in,
Only to get Nibbles.
Pieces of bait fall away,
of Games You Play.
Only to Dangle Possibility.

Tried to stay away,
Added more Bait.
Came Running back,
Hooked & Pulling.
I ended it all,
The Games Cut the line.
Permanently Scarred,
Bleeding for,
What Introduced to Me.

Twisted

Sarcastic & Hypocritical,
Self Centered, Back Stabbing,
Self Righteous Little.

How I Can't Stand.

Sweet & Graceful,
Loyal & Devoted,

How Do I Love.
Each Breath,
Cause of You.

Unbound

Of me,
They Need no more.
For Them,
No longer a Reason.
Possessions Mean Nothing.
Heart is Torn,
Tears of Sadness Hidden.
Laws or Rules,
I Played By No one's.
Taste,
Of Love I've Forgotten.

1st Impression

Your Love Shone Down,
Kept away from Me.
Like a Virus,
A Disease,
Impatient to receive.
Out from Under.
Please,
Introduce Me.

Close

Though we Lay
Sweaty Bodies Entangled
With word Unspoken.
Small Town rumors
Louder than anything we could Say
Contemplating our actions
Avoiding to hurt one another
Praying for the phone to ring.

Left Path

Behind these Eyes,
I know all to well,
Glaring Stare,
Hiding Tears fall.
Ecstasy when You're to Me.
On Finger a Ring should be.
Situation way it was,
Destined to go,
Life's Devastation,
Lead separate roads.

A Glimpse

In the car,
Daughter in back.
Summertime Boston Market,
A Beautiful Little Girl In Cute outfit,
A Breathtaking Woman,
In the Driver's Seat.
Passenger with Melancholy Grin
That Moment, Tis Simplistic,
Always with Me.

Journey

Temptation of one's Pleasures
Through a soul's deceit
Embark by ones Fate
Hopes of Dreams Twisted by Karma
Feelings of a Transparent Looking Glass
Past Journey regretful
An image of burning desire
Promising future
Sensationally Yours

Released

As Asked, It is Done
Much aware of what this is
Still abiding
Pleading to be the One
The one, to each other
Yielded by Sexual Enlightenment
Trapped by responsibility
Partake Amnesty in Seduction
Of One's Heart.

Asked

A Thousand Stories,
One Look on a face.
Nor Deceiver Nor Lie,
Told Look in a Pair of Eyes.
Prominent Discussion,
Glorious or Tragic Outcome,
Insurmountable odds,
Prominently asked Question,
Will You Marry me?

House Abandoned '04

To this day it awaits,
no pictures hung in the hall,
pieces of glass on the floor,
closets with still hangers,
new dust covered appliances,
furnished rooms yet to be touched.

Said you wanted all,
security, house, significant other.
these lies never saw,
a believer I was.
a family,
a life I never known,
as I promised,
13 Room House quiet street,
Children's swing set in yard,
no curtains to draw nor Doors to lock,
accounts well off,
Author position I hold,

This perfect Soccer Mom's Life,
always you wanted,
just,
not with me.

Even though

When You call upon Me,
I'll tell you all the things
You want to Hear.
I'll pick You up when
You're Feeling Down,
I fix Your Problems,
When You need Me,
Mental , Physical,
No matter for What,
Even when You're in Fear,
I do for You,
I'm there for You,
Your Significant Other,
You call on Me
Even though I'm Alone Inside,
No matter I'll be Here.

Reasons

Sorry I told You the Truth.
Sorry I was there for You.
Sorry I wanted a Life with You.
Sorry I quit everything for You.
Sorry I betrayed & Turned
My back on Family,
Because of You , For You.
Sorry I wanted Everything with you
Sorry I am not Sorry,
Not Sorry at All.

Spoken

Tell me You Like Me,
Tell Me You Want Me,
Tell Me You Feel Like a Woman,
Because of Me.

Cheat on your Husband,
Lie to Him.

Tell Me You Want
To Be With Me,
Find any Excuse to See Me,
Find any Excuse To Be With Me.

Realizing I am Your Dream of a Fantasy,
Divorce Your Husband,
Now Scared it could be True.

Tell Me Don't Touch Me,
Tell Me We Need a Break,
Tell Me We're Just Friends,
Tell Me You Want Security.
Your Games, Lies
The Continuous Betrayal.

Tell You I'm In Love With You,
Your Child as My Own,
With Me for ME Or Security,?

Tell Me Why You Are Scared.
Emerald

Misguided & Fault-full,
Treacherous & Deviant,
Lost My Self,
When I Feel for You,
Like Emeralds,
Minor Abrasions & Slight Scarring,
Absolutely Beautiful You Wear,
Like A Pay Check,
Hard to Earn,
Quick to Lose.

Burning

Slayed down upon Your Feet,
Ambitions Burn like a Creeping Fire,
Past Relationships Smothering Intent,
Waiting for Your Answer,
Like an Oxygen Starved Flame,
Smoldering, Waiting,
As to Flash Bright with the next Breath,
It was meant as a Option,
A Chance if You Will,
Enthusiastically Reigniting,
All the Temptations Of
Things I Want to do to You,
The Things I Want to do with You.

Broken Promise

Never laughed when You Fell,
Stood by Your Side,
Reassuring Kept Will.

Tried to be there,
Give You a House to call Home.
Give You Security.

Promised I'd always be there for You.
Promised I'd never Hurt You.
To Protect Your Innocence.

Thought you Were an Angel sent to Me,
Asked for Your Loyalty,
Your Devotion.

Replied Scared & Conflicted.

To Protect My Heart,
Broke Thy Promises,
I'm Sorry
To Protect You From Me,
I Walked Away.

Restrain

Lost in Emotions,
Trapped by Love,
Bounded by friendship,
Time with each other,
Neither will ever forget.
Ending You & I,
Best thing I could Do,
I Miss You.

Confession

I've Practiced so many times,
A never ending migraine I now have.
Till this day,
A lie to you,
I've never done.
Hope was lost on me.
Happiness as fleeting moments.
Taste of your lips,
Not unlike subduction.
A smile lighting up the darkness,
Encasing my life.
More than a friendship,
Never a relationship.
A Dream life with you,
My fantasy never to come true.
Infatuations of the past,
I fell In Love with you.
I hold no resentment,
Nor Hard feelings.
This is true,
Every thing I only wish for you.
Found myself still thinking of you.

Of You

Your Kisses are Poison
Becoming, addicted a little more each time.
Your touch,
That of amber's,
softly burning my skin
Making me visibly unappealing.
Your voice cuts through me
Stripping away the wall I've built
With every emotional wound.
The sweet flirtatious looks
Keep me at a painful attention.
The gentle way of you
Leaves me craving more.
For of you I'm falling.

Simplicity

Soft, smooth,
sateen
to touch,
the feel of a woman's skin.
The way she smells,
softness of her hair.
That sparkle,
brightness in her eyes.
Like a feather,
soft delicate touch of her hand
sliding from my cheek,
Down my neck,
over my collar bone
settles on my chest as she falls asleep.
At ease comfortably lost
watching her sleep,
my breath escapes.

The Way You

Curious,
By the Look in Your Eyes.
Intrigued,
By Your Panache.
Tempted,
By the Natural Aroma of Thee.
Aroused Physically,
By Your Touch.
Stimulated,
By Our Conversation.
Eager,
Getting to Know You.

Some Day

Candle Light the way,
Across Drifting Waters I Lay.
Deviated in, Protection of.
Rumor told nothing more,
Comeback to see
Safe & Well without me.
Can I handle
To see You again,
When I say,
I'M Sorry.

Left

If I gave You what You Need,
Hiding My Desires.
Deception,
Beaten within,
Failed to belong to any one,
Protected; by losing You
True as it be,
Only left,
Demons within Me.

Talked

fell in love
mastered a carrier
now with a comfortable life
I told her my past,
5 & 1/2 yrs, all in all
It could not last
Lost to the
darkness inside & my past.
So my life has become my work
19 long year career
Tis now over
Retired & empty
void & bored
Like time, all things come to pass
Tis the cost for who I once was.
no heart left & my mind I've lost.
Time to time
Think
I miss her .
I hope her heart's content.

Purity

A Smile,
That which Burns One's Soul.
Lighting,
The Darkest Place of a Heart.
Eyes of Innocence,
From every Angle,
Tearing,
Invoked & Bound,
Distraught Riddle of,
A Graceful Essence.
What is of a Woman?
Of You ?

Almost

Spoken upon Once,
Argued about Daily.
Can't except the past,
Nor let it go,
For a Future.
Promised You.
Never to be Hurt,
Never let you see that Life,
Never to have it hinder,
Our life...
Your doubt,
Now Hinders all that is Us.
Your fear of Me,
My Past &,
Fear of what you feel.
Ends You & I.
Now Loss for both of Us,
Of what we almost had.

Infliction

simplicity of chivalry,
becomes an insult
soft caress of her hand,
delightedly torturous
sweat taste of moist lips,
a never ending craving
sound of her voice,
nails on a chalk board
sex with one you choose,
now a project to get some
waking up to her again,
nearly unbearable
to stay, a nightmare
to break up, to leave her
miserable you'll be.

Even

Treated You as You Should
Be Treated.
Disrespected Me,
Spit in my Face,
Treated Me as a Friend.

Abrupt conversation & state of cold,
What You received from Me,
I'm Entitled to Your Dismay.

Sold '09

Tried to fill it,
with a Wife,
Children to make it a home.

furnished waiting to be used,
dream life of a Family fantasy,
never to be a place,
called home.

5 yrs waited
to stop the hurt.
to dream no more.
fantasy failed.
abandoned,
Now sold,

An Abandoned House no more.

Patients

Scars, Left in their wake
Memories, Wishing they were fake
Sorrow, For word spoken
Ache, Wear Heart once Touched
Untrusting, For which time Betrayed
Tears fall Inside, Still I hide
Patients Please,
From those came before You
I'M no longer just Neurotic
I'M Broken
Damaged Goods left behind.

Photo

for you to never stray,
be held gentle with firm support,
ritual words for your heart to convey ,
in your darkest hour of enlightenment,
of your Beauty only an image could portray.

Catcher

Words caught my interest,
Image has become my Muse,
like a spell Compassion enlightens,
Essence keeps me returning for more abuse,
dreams being thy only security.

in my thoughts,
intentions, & of my desire,
Eager for more as you're,
wielding a Dream catcher,
you have all that is not damaged.

awake with thought of your Grace,
day becomes a soft kiss of a gentle,
summer's breeze,
a perfume hint of garden Roses,
could you want of me?

Seductive

Your hand delicately brushes my hair,
Your palm against my cheek soft as the first
Snowflake,
My heart jumps as if chimes in the air,
Startling me so that I cling to you for fear,
Falling off a never ending cliff,
As I choke from losing my breath.

Depth of pain 'n' sorrow,
Intensity of desire, & passion,
longing for understanding 'n'
acknowledgment,
In-between moments of solace,
Told within your stare,
Waiting for emotions to have spoken words.

Touch of your fingers grazing mine,
Delicate as a single drop of wine,
Rolling it around I savor it on my tongue,
Try to make it last forever.

Plea of Reason

While laying aching & annoyed,
Set aside your doubts, Your fears,
Your contradicting mind,
Morbid Inhibitions of Discreet Insurrection.
leave it written in the book of Torment.
Ye of Suspenseful Pleasures,
Tis a Muse I found in thous morning plea.

It is I whom called you down,
Curiously intrigued,
Painful twisted Life of Romance,
As my breath escapes me.
I awake to find a Goddess,
Reading our words on a Blessed Day.

If Only

Sadistic life; lived,
pain overflowing,
Nothing worth striving for,
Darkness consumed,
Disappointment bleeding; from every seam,
Wrapped in agony; In a web of Deceit,
No intentions remain,
Torment of emptiness; in everything seen,
Tried to hid; left sadistically confined.
Tears; of an empty heart,
Hope; but a fantasy,
Cursed by the Gods,
Kindred Soul; Only myself to thank,
longing all; Please End.

Intentions

Courses among life's routine,
Inner-strength seen in structure,
Purity of a hindered heart told in hazle eyes,
Gentle persuasion of fingertips grazing mine,
Smile of interest,
Seemingly amused 'n' compelled by curiosity,
If only to know each-other.

You Left

You said,
Lock me away in your prison,
Throw away the key,
So I'll never be free.
I said,
I didn't love you,
Don't want you, Don't need you.

When you cried, I crumbled inside.
You walked out, Just left without a fight.
Disappeared from my sight.

I lied.
I am in love with you,
I want you, I need you,
Emptiness of me, you once completed.
Impatiently waiting, Please come back,

Back to me.

ODE to Waiting

Full lips; taste of wine,
Intristic of heart's mending,
Resting on winged back of a black soul.
Tortuously seducing a sadistic tease,
Distant memories of past lives lived,
Sweet succulent aroma of mutual Orgasms.
Flavor in pleasure of desire,
Innocent acts wheeling,
Anticipation in Angst.
Whispers craving more,
As body's yearning to ravish.
Restricted ambitions led by thee unobtainable,
holding out with a purpose for something
true.

Drawn In

Virtues of a woman,
Of charismatic reputation,
Intrinsic intentions,
Wanting control as a Dominatrix,
Unique personality with intelligence,
Hot bodied with a Passion of lust,
Man's last request, Trust.

Thy Woman's Body

That of a silky flower's petal,
Sensual movements of just so,
How I can spend hours,
Feeling the contour of her.

Alluring facial expressions,
Baring eyes telling an emotional story,
Subtly encouraging me to abide,
How I can spend hours,
Lost in her gaze.

Ever so gentle tease of succulent juices,
Flowing from within full plump lips,
How I can Spend hours,
Still leaves me an unquenchable thirst.

Strong tongue speaking words, Unsure.
Such a persuasive sound in a voice,
How I can spend hours,
She refrains,
Compelling one to pursue.

Between Us

In case I forget to tell you,
In case I forgot to say,
Read this to start your day.

I haven't seen the future,
Nothing is written in stone,
I'm looking forward to seeing where this can
go.

(Placed on the counter; in front of the coffee
pot,
Lays this note; where you'll see it for sure.
The days I forget to tell you,
When I forgot to say,
Read this to start your day.
I'm interested 'n' this feeling's yet to stray.)

I think we fell into something,
Which looks to be a good run,
This isn't over; we've only just begun.
I've traced your Tattoos with my tongue,
Awake to you beside me, occasionally in my
arms.

(If I'm gone before you awake,
On the counter; in front of the coffee pot,
Lays this note; where you'll see it for sure.
In case I forget to tell you,
In case I forgot to say,

Read this to start your day.
I'm interested 'n' this feelings increases
everyday.)

We may not see eye to eye,
We may argue time to time.
Push 'n' tempt each other,
Communication, sex, trust, loyalty, devotion,
Yet to be a Lie.

(Place this note back on the counter,
As a gentle reminder to start your day.
I'm interested 'n' eager to awake,
If only, to see you each day.)

Last Night's 1 month Toast:

When my mind stops my mouth,
from saying what my heart feels,
allow this evening to speak for it.

What to do?

Whence they meet,
attracted by appearance,
attracted by curiosity,
attracted.
Pursue relationship,
alleged commitment to each-other,
yet not Boyfriend / Girlfriend to one-a-other.
Introduced as Man I'm Dating / Boyfriend,
as I introduce as Woman I'm Dating /
Girlfriend.
find I'm falling,
What is a Man suppose to do?

A phone call, a guy never spoken of.
Told him, I'm a friend.
Days fly, a lunch date she has on her mind.
Quickly to get off phone, as he walks to her
car.,
for her date not to know.
What is a Man suppose to do?

Conversations begin,

Arguments ensue there after.
Continuously told: slow down, not yet, back
up,
I'm not sure about you,
What is a Man suppose to do?

A Laborer with a questionable past,
a Past of all he really knows.
A Woman sickened by what's told.
Arguments ensue.
He stays 'n' argues, for he's fallen for you.
What is a Man suppose to do?

A Kiss, & if you want; call,
then I walk out the door.

What I want,
What I've been looking for,
Potential of Possibility,
still I'm falling
hands down, no contest,
you're a better person than me, by far.
You're not sure what you want
& all I want is with you.
So tell me,
What is a Man suppose to do?

Memory of Thy One

Met someone new, Future I pursue.
Memories; rush back to you,
Things we would do,
Conversations ensue arguments,
Of no purpose nor reason.

Touch her skin, Finger tips grazing mine.
Kiss her lips, Sweet as a a drop of wine.
Soft words caressing each other's longing,
Yet I wish it was with you.

Went to the mall, a clothing show she put on.
Caught in thought, all I see is you.
Store is no more, of your ring I had bought.
Awkward, I slipped and mentioned you.

Days, weeks, months, 'n' Yrs gone by,
To forget her, Still I try.
How you laughed, Tears you've cried.
The undecidable look behind your eyes.
The way you'd carry your self,
High Maintenance,
You; I should have kept.

I wish I could find the words to say,
How I wish you would've stayed.

I left the life,
The only life I ever knew, For you.
I long of your seducing kiss,
The comfort within your arms embrace.
The belief, the confidence you had in me.

I find myself reminiscing,
It feels like it was yesterday.

How I wish,
I didn't miss you to this day.

With in a:

Though full of restrain,
Passion 'n' desire burns through.
Hindered by the pain she feels,
Longing for her own.
Oh to be, for her.

What wonders of divination,
Lay behind those eyes,
In a stare that could stop a heart,
Oh how I get lost every time.

Smooth 'n' soft of a flowers peddle,
Thous skin glistens as if glowing.
Luscious moist lips,
Yearning to be kissed.
I think I'm falling,
for your vibrant yet subtle look of,
Innocence.

Ending Effervescence

Seven hrs embellished,
In mutual sexual satisfaction.
Last nights sordid affair,
Left aching, Panting in exhaustion,
As the sun rays
Kissed our glistening bodies.

Irreconcilable

As she was to me,
I've felt only once before.
Mistakes we've both made.
Deceptive; Indecisive,
Sheltered both claim to be.
Honest I was,
Ignorant to her views,
Being truthful was our undoing.

Both came to say,
Fell back; a slave to their ex.
Questioning themselves,
Look to me for a sense of security.
Mutual regret & sincerity,
Hopeful I'd be there,
To be what they need,
Regain feeling of a Woman.
Opened myself,
Subjected to mental cruelty,
No longer shall I grieve.

Collaboration

Breaths of panting
Sweating; head to toe
Emotional moaning
Grunting
Thighs spread
Lips open wide
Penetration ensues
Nails digging deeper
Thrusting deeper
Bodies entangled
No end, only a satisfaction sigh
Lost recollection of time
Heart, Mind, Body, verbal expression
All in perfect rhythm
A physical rhyme

Thy Own

Fragrance; hints to a past conquest
Voice; rush memories of a once love
Dreams; hunted by Faces of victims
Heart; weighted by Dolor of Romance
Life; restricted by Truculent experiences
Mind; bound by Adjy of society
Time spent without conscious
Equally spent with knowing
Entangled; prison of my own doing
Awaiting; experience of Befall
Will you please release me?

Of Hope

From whence we were in such love,
Thus the comfort of memory,
Though; I shutter the thought.
Please do not speak of it,
Thy heart can't bear to listen to my ears.

Even if it were wrong, I'd stay.

Claiming to want what we once had,
Love that we once knew.
No longer possess the strength,
To walk away from that which
I've longed for to be new.

You'll have to be the one to end it.

Secrets; there are none,
Of yours, I care not to know.
Mythic story of love, war and loss.
Filled with hope.
Inevitably; a sorrowful ending.

Fit For a King

Acknowledgment 'n' loyalty
Given unto me graciously,
Enforced by fear.
That which can not be spoken of, a past.
Thy soul's retribution, unobtainable.
Haunted by the life I once knew
Longing for the quiet, a happy medium.

Rotting mansion for a house.
Equity 'n' principal abundant.
Financial stability accomplished.
Resting on Home & Garden's cover.
Value of thy continued breath, 0.
Thy kin, millions; when my demise.

Journey unexpected, yet none for granted.
10yr plan, seemingly thwarted.
Still missing a wife 'n' children

Notions of man,
Feeling of love is transcending,
Though the act of love remains tangible.
To a woman,
Love is given freely and turned to hatred easily
Shown by the suffering we inflict upon each
other.
Lavished & spoiled though we may become,
Feeble we remain.
Risking our jobs, our livelihood in which we
obtain
Through blood sweat & tears.
Eagerly willing to risk one's life,
In order to protect the ones we love.
Ultimately showing the lengths we'll go
through
Over an emotion found, once in a lifetime.

Bereave

Fell in love with an amazing woman,
I could not have.
Twisted words of pain,
When we parted.
Friendship lost,
That of one, I've never known.
The likes of, I will never have again.
Chance of happiness,
Caused our end.

Trapped Solitude

Looks you given me,
Formed planks on both sides.
Your actions anchored them to the floor.
Your e-mail became a lid to cover me.
Words you've spoken, like nails driven in.
Broken; gasping for air to breath.
In this coffin you've built around me.

Entranced

Inside the shine of a crest glow,
Beckoning to the whim of the night.
Into the gaze of the crow,
Humbly she stares,
Understanding what she sees.
Feeling the sorrow,
Carried on the winged back of the crow.
Inescapable essence, she loses herself.
Eagerly willing to join
An old soul's journey to the next life.

January Morning

Look up to the sky
curse the morning that is new
clouds of snow and rain
hovering above
Three feet of snow below
sun burning through
yearning to lavish its glow on you
from whence the night held such promise
for the end to be true
for the end to be near
Shoveling & snow blowing
What a way to start a new yr.

More

I wish I could say that the words you've said
make a difference in my head
though I'm thick headed
my dignity is abundant
though confident, my self-esteem is little to
none
my old beliefs allow me the ignorance of my
virtues
each tryst exploratory or not
adds a little more wax beneath my kindled
flame
feelings for you I do not know
I wish I could say your actions
make a difference to me
more than it is, a future you request of me
each exploit of voyeurism
I enjoy you more then the last
though you're not the one
anything more you will never be
leading you on for my own gratification
I apologize

However

thy hart tainted
my will abundant
I've rode the serpent
kissed the goddess of death
yet I remain broken 'n' breathing
only two regrets
oddly, I'm satisfied

As Close

to dance with another
won't happen
someone decent
settle-down, raise a family
would be to pacify me
the friendship we had I'll never know again
secrets I had none
tears we had both shed
no one will ever know me as you have
you were the one
no one will ever come as close
best part of my life was you
I only wish you could forgive me

Once Felt

you make me feel high above everything
like i could take on & conquer anything
nothing could hold me back
nothing could stop me
feeling of this I've never known before
have never known since
how is it you managed to do this
how is it you made me fall in love with you

A Chance

if I'm meant to live a life without you
I'll try to make the best of it
feelings I still bear
sorry for the resentment you may still harbor
I've abandoned the only life I ever knew
turned my back on family to
for a chance to have any type of
future life with you

I'm Now

changed who I was and my life
just to be worthy
just to be with you
fell into a downward spiral
lost myself when I lost you
time gone by 'n' I realize
I've become the man you deserve
still I try to be who you knew I could be
till the day we meet again
I can only hope you'll see
I am now the man
you always knew I could be

My Heart

I find myself missing
longing for what my heart once knew
the way you held my hand
how you stood beside me
never to walk behind me
how your lip curls as you truly smile
the way your hair shimmers
like a sunny wheat field in Clinton
soothing voice with a face of an angel
a body to die for 'n' a
intoxicating natural smell
my backbone you became
I see now I'm still missing
longing for what my heart once knew

Please Know

that of which I thought I once knew
I've come to learn my virtues
where the only thing ever true.
everything you do
seems to be plotted
meticulous manipulative scam
planned & graciously executed
every step of the way
when I fell for you
I played the part of a fool quite well
understanding I now have
of why things were & why things are
though I strive to be for you
a simple friendship just won't do
if you come back please know this
my heart has always been true

Among

bask in the glory of the moon's light
bathed in the black of the night
before you I never knew
warmth of the sun 'n' the grace of the day
with a dark cloud 'n' a gray soul
I relished & thrived
with you the clouds dissipated
light cast down through
it filled me & empowered me
to be a god among ordinary people
a privilege I only experienced because of you

My Wish

find my self
remembering, reminiscing
of a life i once lived
the things I used to do
how I once was
before & through the first yr of us
to this new life I've grown accustomed
which was introduced by you to me
I only regret it's no longer with you
still I'm haunted by my past
I wish I could let go of it
as you have of me

Authors Published Work's

Dolor; UN-edited poetry, 1st. edition. Print

Dine and Dash; 10 minute dinner recipes.
Print and eBook/ePub

Eluded Confession; realistic thriller novel.
Print and eBook/ePub

Stuckey's Venison Recipes.
Print and eBook/ePub

Dolor; Deceived by Love. Poetry, 2nd. edition
Print and eBook/ePub

Adjy; Poetry, 1st. edition.
Print and eBook/ePub

Truculent; poetry, 1st. edition.
Print and eBook/ePub

Main Website: Author-MStuckey.com

www.ingramcontent.com/pod-product-compliance
Lightning Source LLC
Chambersburg PA
CBHW051903090426
42811CB00003B/439